Coaching and Wheatsheaf Inn

23 Load Street, Bewdley

Dedicated to all my family, especially to my late Mother and maternal Grandmother, who spent many happy holidays in Bewdley throughout their lives and who, with my Father, introduced me to Bewdley. Also to my late maternal Great Grandfather, John Cornforth, a foreman at Tangye Brothers' Cornwall Works, Smethwick, for many years.

Coaching and the Wheatsheaf Inn

23 Load Street, Bewdley

Sue Brown

HiP
HISTORY INTO PRINT

First published by
History Into Print, 56 Alcester Road,
Studley, Warwickshire B80 7LG in 2010
www.history-into-print.com

ISBN: 978-1-85858-332-7

A Cataloguing in Publication Record
for this title is available from the British Library.

Typeset in Baskerville
Printed in Great Britain by
Hobbs the Printers Ltd.

CONTENTS

Acknowledgements   viii

Abbreviations   ix

Illustrations and Press Cuttings   x

Preface   xii

Introduction: If Only He Could Speak   xiii

1   A Brief History of Bewdley's Wheatsheaf Inn   1

2   Coaching   10

3   Coaching in Bewdley before 1835   18

4   The Heyday of Coaching at the Wheatsheaf   24

    Appendix: Some of the Wheatsheaf's Other Roles   33

    Notes and References   36

Bewdley Institute as it is today. Photograph: David W. Brown, 2003.

TITLES IN THIS SERIES

1. 'Over Agaynst the Chappell': 21-23 Load Street, Bewdley
   – the Buildings and Occupants from *c*1632 to *c*1875
2. Coaching and the *Wheatsheaf Inn*, 23 Load Street, Bewdley
3. Bewdley Institute, 21-23 Load Street: a Sketch from
   *c*1875 to *c*1950
4. Bewdley Institute, 21-23 Load Street: Founder Edward
   Pease (1834-1880) and Some of his Associates

ACKNOWLEDGEMENTS

I owe a great deal to the late Dr. David Lloyd, M.B.E., M.A., original tutor of Bewdley Historical Research Group, whose expertise and enthusiasm inspired me, and to all members of the Group, past and present. I am especially indebted to Mr. Bob Tolley, B.Sc.(Hons.), Dipl.Arch., R.I.B.A. – Bewdley born and bred – for his architectural advice and expertise; to former *Stewards* Tim who allowed Bob and me to explore the inside and the back of the Bewdley Institute building and to Mr. & Mrs. David Carr and the late Mr. Bob Gawne; to Mr. A. Ashcroft, Mrs. J. Keane, and Mr. Bill Sedgeley for their help; to the Institute Committee for allowing me to reproduce the photograph of the building; to Mr. & Mrs. C. J. Bond for an 1870s photograph of the *Wheatsheaf;* to the Society of Antiquaries of London for allowing me to reproduce W. & J. Lewis's trade card of the Royal Sovereign Day Coach; to the British Postal Museum & Archive for permission to reproduce a photograph of the first Mail Coach, 1784; to Mr. David Edwards for allowing me to reproduce his painting *Midsummer Magic* and his drawing of the lamplighter; to English Heritage, National Monuments Record for permission to include their photograph of part of Leycester's Hospital in Warwick High Street; to Mrs. Jan Ferguson for showing me an 1871 drawing of 21-23 Load Street by A. E. Everitt and to the Birmingham Museums and Art Gallery for allowing me to reproduce it; to staff of the Reference Libraries at Birmingham and Kidderminster and of Worcestershire County Record Office; to Mr. Peter White of Darlington Library & Art Gallery; to David & Charles, Publishers; to *Berrow's Worcester Journal* and the *Kidderminster Shuttle/Times*; to Mr. David Finch; to my husband, David, for his photographs; and last, but not least, to my family for helping solve computer problems, for checking my typescript and for putting up with me during twenty-odd years of research on the complex of buildings which is known today as Bewdley Institute, numbers 21-23 Load Street.

Sue Brown
March 2009

ABBREVIATIONS

B.H.R.G.	Bewdley Historical Research Group
D.N.B.	Dictionary of National Biography
I.G.I.	International Genealogical Index
K.S.	*Kidderminster Shuttle*
K.T.	*Kidderminster Times*
M.C.R.	Manor Court Rolls/Records
S.O.E.D.	Shorter Oxford English Dictionary
V.C.H.	(Salop) Victoria History of the County of Shropshire
V.C.H.	(Worcs.) Victoria History of the County of Worcestershire
W.R.O.	Worcestershire County Record Office

ILLUSTRATIONS AND PRESS CUTTINGS

1870s *Sepia Photograph of the Wheatsheaf*, Front cover
by kind permission of Mr. & Mrs. C. J. Bond

Midsummer Magic: Back cover
Artist: David Edwards – a coach in Load Street

Bewdley Institute as it is today: vi
Photograph: David W. Brown, 2003

The Carved Mask: xiii
Photograph: David W. Brown, 1980s

Photograph of part of *Leycester's Hospital in Warwick High Street*, 3
taken by G. B. Mason, 1942. © English Heritage, National
Monuments Record and reproduced by their kind permission

1870s *Sepia Photograph of the Wheatsheaf*, 6
by kind permission of Mr. & Mrs. C. J. Bond

Load Street, July 1871 from *Town and Country* 7
in the West Midlands: the Watercolours and Drawings
of A. E. Everitt of Birmingham 1824-1882,
Birmingham Museums and Art Gallery [B.M.A.G.], 1986
© B.M.A.G. and reproduced by their kind permission

Two Advertisements for the *Sale of the Wheatsheaf* 8-9
One reproduced by kind permission of *Berrow's Worcester Journal*

The Reader at the Plough, Kidderminster. 13
Reproduced from Edward Broadfield's
Guide to Kidderminster & Neighbourhood.
Printed by W. Hepworth, 1889.

Some *Press Cuttings about Highwaymen, Road Conditions, etc.*   14-16
Three reproduced by kind permission of *Berrow's Worcester Journal*

Signboard of what may have been the former   17
Highwayman Café in Stourport Road, Bewdley,
illus. by Sydney H. Jones, *c*1950s

W. & J. Lewis's Trade Card for the *Royal Sovereign Day Coach*   21
© The Society of Antiquaries, London and reproduced
by their kind permission

1784 illustration of the First Mail Coach   22
© The British Postal Museum & Archive, London
and reproduced by their kind permission

The Lamplighter Outside the Wheatsheaf, c1870   31
Artist's impression, David Edwards, 2003

Ann Allcott's Billhead, the Wheatsheaf, 1856 courtesy B.H.R.G.   35

PREFACE

Bewdley Historical Research Group was founded in 1981 by Mavis Barrett, who suggested the idea, Kenneth Hobson, Angela and Charles Purcell and Sue Brown and derived from the nucleus of an original Birmingham Extramural Class held in 1971/1972.

In addition to gathering information on all aspects of the history of the town, each member has a particular area of work or specific responsibility. My charge is to co-ordinate data on buildings on the south and west sides of Load Street. By using the facts gathered by all the members over the years, including myself, I have compiled this and other accounts as preliminary sketches of a building which, perhaps, is under-rated today, but which historic records and architectural evidence show was very important. Although as complete as I can make these studies from the records examined so far, i.e. from *c*1660-*c*1950, they are not intended to be definitive histories of either the complex of buildings or its occupants. Neither do they purport to represent anything but my own interpretation. Any errors and omissions, etc., are entirely my responsibility and I would be grateful for constructive criticism and additional information.

Figures given in brackets after any sums of money quoted in pounds, shillings & pence represent the approximate equivalent in decimal currency, rounded up or down to the nearest penny except where I felt that a more direct comparison was needed, although, of course, a true comparative *value* of money then and now is very difficult to make.

To avoid an excessively long list of references, where none is cited I have taken the information from the Manor Court Rolls.

Although properties in Bewdley were not given street numbers until towards the end of the 19th century, for the sake of simplicity the present-day numbering is used in this text except where otherwise indicated. So, too, are today's street names.

INTRODUCTION: IF ONLY HE COULD SPEAK

Bewdley lies on the west bank of the Severn in Worcestershire and the river played a major part in the life of the settlement for centuries. The *Wheatsheaf*, a timber-framed building, is located in Bewdley's main street in what was the centre of a busy market place in the seventeenth century. A carved mask looks down from the angle of the building's bargeboards. If only he could speak, then what wonderful tales he could tell of times past and of coaching days in the town. Known as the *Wheatsheaf* between *c*1754 and *c*1875, today the premises form the west end of Bewdley Institute, currently numbered 21-23 Load Street.

By 1788 number 23 was established as the *Wheatsheaf*, one of two principal inns – the other being the longer-established and larger *George* on the opposite side of the road.[1]

Detail from the gable of number 23 Load Street. Beneath the date 1632 are the initials W^MB. Photograph: David W. Brown, 1980s.

In 1875 Edward Pease, Esq., of Darlington purchased the *Wheatsheaf* and neighbouring buildings on the site in this study. Later, he gave the premises to the town as an educational and recreational Institute, subject to a small chief rent and a small payment to Bewdley Grammar School.[2]

Bewdley Institute was officially opened to both sexes in 14th October 1878. The middle section of the complex seems to have originally consisted of two buildings or of one building divided internally into two. For ease of reference, the eastern part of this central section will be referred to as number 22a and the western part as number 22b.

At some time between 1875 and 1878 numbers 21 and 22a had been "pulled down or converted" to render them suitable for use as the Institute. It was probably during this refurbishment that the entry was moved eastwards from the original site in the area of 22b, nowadays Hayden's Estate Agent's, to its present location between numbers 21 and 20, the latter being today's shop known as 'Bewdley Books'.

Currently the Institute premises house a Club, a gentlemen's hairdressers, an estate agent's and a meeting room. In addition, regular activities such as pétanque, table tennis, yoga, judo and weightwatchers take place on the site.

This brief study aims to give a flavour of coaching nationally and to show something of the role of Bewdley's *Wheatsheaf* therein.

Chapter One

A BRIEF HISTORY OF BEWDLEY'S WHEATSHEAF INN

From Bakery to Inn

Before being adapted to form part of the Institute, number 23 Load Street had been a bakery for about 24 years, where **Thomas Weaver** was the baker from *c*1693[3]-*c*1717, and an inn from *c*1754-c1875. Was it Thomas who adopted the trade sign of the bakers, the wheatsheaf, to advertise his business there?

What an apt name for a building which, in the 17th century, stood near markets for corn, barley and malt – the staple ingredients of the end-products of both trades.

Bread, long regarded as 'the staff of life' and water as 'the wine of life', it is interesting to speculate on the relationship between them and the bread and wine of the Eucharist at the 15th century wooden chapel[4] whose door stood "over agaynst" number 23 until *c*1745 – and, perhaps, on the central location of both church and market in towns in general. The heart of life indeed.

The first *record* by the name of **'the Wheatsheaf'** seems to have occurred in *c*1754[5] and, indeed, in *c*1750 a Corporation Rent Book referred to the premises as **'Houses late Weavers'**.

Conceivably, though, number 23 might have *become* an inn about twenty years earlier, for **in 1734** two men with the name **Thomas Bodenham** had appeared on a list of **Victuallers' Recognizances**[6] – one being an *innholder*, the other a *sadler* (sic). Could one of them have been the Thomas Bodenham who had been copyholder (tenant of the lord of the manor) of number 22b in *c*1743 and of number 23 at his death in *c*1753?

Interestingly, the 1753 description of number 23 indicates that it had reverted to being "one messuage or tenement", instead of the two recorded in 1739. The premises no longer included a *bakehouse*, but a *brewhouse* was listed. It was fairly common for people to have a brewhouse at that time, so too much significance should not be attached to this *first known mention* of one at number 23, but the description also includes an outhouse, as well as the "backside" mentioned in 1717 and "outbuildings" of 1739, suggesting expansion of the premises behind number 23.

A **Richard Northall**, another baker, was also recorded on the **1734 Recognizances**. Could he have been the Richard Northall of the Northall family who, although they may never have lived there, **mortgaged number 23 to John Jefferys**, (gent.) of Franch (sic) for £250 plus interest **in 1780** when they **inherited** the premises **from Ann(e) Bodenham**, widow of Thomas Bodenham? John Jefferys[7] and his oldest son Matthew are listed in Bailey's Directory for 1783 as "millers and mealmen" – appropriate successors to a baker.

In **1786** Matthew Jefferies (sic) (gent.) of Kidderminster inherited the premises. By this time **David Rowland** held the lease. If David Rowland had taken this up in 1776, when numbers 21, 22a and 22b had been surrendered to his use, then he would appear to be *the first occupant of all the property on this site* during the period under review. Rowland also seems to be the first *recorded* innholder or victualler *of the premises*.

Regarding the evolution of the *Wheatsheaf* during the time of Thomas Weaver (senior), baker, it is worth offering here an interesting, although somewhat tentative, hypothesis. Nothing in Thomas's Inventory, 1717,[8] indicated that he ever combined baking with brewing, but it did mention "Bowen's House" – although where it was located is not clear. "Bowen's House" appeared to contain simply "15 chairs and stools and 1 oval table", appraised at £1-2s-0d. (£1.10). Surely, this was rather a large number of chairs and stools for a house? *If it were situated in the yard behind* number 23, then could "Bowen's House" have been the forerunner of the *Wheatsheaf* and if "Bowen" was the ***Rowland* Bowen,** joyner, (sic) listed in **Victuallers' and Alehouse Keepers' Recognizances** for **1734**, then could he have been the *premises' first* innholder? On the other hand, if "Bowen's House" *had been occupied,* but perhaps not lived in, by *Rowland* Bowen then, as a joiner, he may have made the furniture himself and simply stored it there. As noted elsewhere, the first *recorded* innholder at number 23 was **David Rowland** in 1776.

On balance, ***it seems quite possible that number 23 developed naturally from baker's shop to inn in c1734,***[9] ***became well-known as the Wheatsheaf from c1752/1753,*** when the new road at Winbrook was made,[10] ***then evolved as a coaching inn after c1776.*** As already observed, David Rowland expanded/altered the premises to include numbers 21, 22a and 22b at some

Photograph of part of Leycester's Hospital in Warwick High Street, taken by G. B. Mason, 1942. This bears similarities to the architectural layout at the back of the Institute. Might the yard behind the Wheatsheaf have looked rather like this after David Rowland's alterations? © English Heritage, National Monuments Record and reproduced by their kind permission.

time between *c*1776-1797. Perhaps his work had been completed well before 1788 and maybe it enabled the inn to conform to what appears to have been a general pattern at that time, i.e. of having an entry from the street leading to a galleried courtyard behind it.[11]

By 1788 the premises included at least two brewhouses and the *Wheatsheaf* had become established as one of Bewdley's two principal inns.

After 1788 the garden seems to have disappeared. *Stables* were built on at least part of it, for an advertisement in *Berrow's Worcester Journal* for 7th February 1788 refers to them – this being the first mention traced so far.

Certainly, there was need for accommodation for horses when the *Wheatsheaf* became a coaching inn. The date 1788 ties in nicely with *both* the demolition and rebuilding work on the site of 21-22b which was undertaken by David Rowland *and* with the clearance of the Shambles from the middle of the street in 1783.[12]

The construction of Telford's bridge, 1798-1801, on a site a few metres north of the Old Bridge[13] straightened out the approach to Bewdley's main street. The removal in *c*1808[14] of the former Court House or Guild Hall which stood immediately in front of today's numbers 24 and 25 Load Street must also have been of great help to the increasing amount of traffic.

After David Rowland's death in *c*1797 his widow and their two daughters were admitted to numbers 21-23 as tenants-in-common. In **1805** they sold to **Humphrey Edwards** of Lyehead; (blank, sic) **Woodward**; and **William Edwards**, oldest son of Humphrey.

Two years later number 23 was described as "now of **Benjamin Giles**". Lewis's Directory for **1820** cites **William Godsall**[15] as "Victualler, *Wheat Sheaf*". Perhaps he was one of the eight, un-named, occupants mentioned there in the 1831 Census, but Pigot's Directory for 1835 records him as "a maltster in High Street".

Bentley's Directory for **1840** named "Thomas Allcock (sic), innkeeper, the *Wheat Sheaf*." The 1841 Census records **Thomas Allcott**'s age as 45 and that of his wife, Ann, as 40 – neither strictly accurate, because the practice at that time was to round adults' ages down to the nearest five years. Their daughter, Elizabeth, was aged 8. All were born in Worcestershire, no town being specified in this Census. **Ann Allcott** succeeded her husband to what was described in **1848** as his "Dwellinghouse", number 23, and she was still listed as being in occupation in **1862**.[16]

Meanwhile, **Thomas Edwards** of Lyehead House, Alton, Rock, yeoman, had inherited number 23 but had died by **1854**, having bequeathed it to his wife, **Sarah**, and then to their son, John. In **1865** this same **John Edwards**, of Middlesex, (gent.) mortgaged number 23 to **William Jones** of Middlesex (gent.) and **Henry William Edwards** of Bewdley (gent.). Another **Weaver**, William, was the tenant at the time. Had he moved to the *George Inn* by 1873?[17]

According to the Census, **John Penn** was the licensed victualler in **1871**,[18] with Henry Hunt, Boot and Shoe Maker, and Amy Milner, Dressmaker, in neighbouring parts of the building, although it is unclear who occupied which part.

James Pearson was recorded as licensee in **1873**,[19] while the Manor Court Records show that the licence of the *Wheatsheaf* was granted to **Mary Richards** in **1874** – although she was recorded there six years earlier.[20]

Mary Pearson, widow of James Pearson?, was in possession of the "messuage with outhouses, brewhouse and buildings" in **1875** when **Henry William Edwards** of Bewdley (gent.) sold the *Wheatsheaf* for £400 to **Edward Pease**, Esq. of Darlington, Co. Durham. As already noted, Mr. Pease afterwards gave these premises – together with numbers 21, 22a and 22b – to the town as Bewdley Institute.

Edward Pease's only child, the Countess of Portsmouth, inherited the premises, being admitted on 23rd December **1887** "by her then description of **Beatrice Mary**, the wife of **Newton Wallop Lymington** (then commonly called Viscount Lymington and now the Rt. Hon. The Earl of Portsmouth)".

The property was enfranchised – freed of obligations to the lord of the manor – in 1902, upon payment of ten guineas (£10.50) and in consideration of a rent charge of 14s-6d. (72.5p) per annum.

The Entry

At some time after 1776 David Rowland demolished a building which stood on the north-east side of the entry to the *Wheatsheaf,* indicating that the entry at that time was on part of the site of today's Hayden's Estate Agent's. In its place he constructed "three new brick buildings" and he "laid the same to the messuage adjoining called the *Wheatsheaf.* The same has ever since (been) part of the *Wheatsheaf.*"

The entry shown in the 1870s photograph (p.6) looks rather narrow, but it was evidently suitable for carriages and coaches **in 1807** because a **conveyance** that year between Hannah Rowland and Humphrey Edwards had "**reserved** … to the said ladies (Hannah and her daughters Hannah and Sarah) and the owners and occupiers … **the right and liberty of a way** … to and from the above said messuages (i.e. numbers 21, 22a and 22b) to Load Street **through and along the yard, entry or passage belonging to the *Wheatsheaf*** as the same has been and is now used **for all purposes** of them and their families, including a right of passage for wheelbarrows and also horses **but not coaches or carriages** from 6.00am to 10.00pm from Michaelmas yearly."

1870s Sepia photograph of the Wheatsheaf, by kind permission of
Mr. & Mrs. C. J. Bond.

Load Street, Bewdley, July 1871 from "Town and Country in the West Midlands: the Watercolours and Drawings of A. E. Everitt of Birmingham 1824-1882", Birmingham Museums and Art Gallery, 1986. © Birmingham Museums and Art Gallery and reproduced by their kind permission.

An illustration made by Mr. A. E. Everitt, an accomplished artist[21], in July 1871 (p.7) shows a lamp projecting over the approach to the *Wheatsheaf* entry and the top of the doorway is horizontal, rather than the arched top which appears on the 1870s photograph.[22] The kerbstone in July 1871 looks flat for the complete length of numbers 21-23, but the 1870s photograph shows a drop-down kerb in front of the entry. There are several other differences between the two illustrations, the 1870s photograph showing steps up to two dilapidated buildings which occupy the site of numbers 21, 22a and 22b and rather nice rounded bay windows to the *Wheatsheaf* and number 22b, whereas Mr. Everitt depicts no steps; angular bay windows; and an attractive gable to number 21. The 1871 Census lists "Page, Samuel (Plumber, Confectioner)" as the occupant of Page's shop which appears on Mr. Everitt's drawing.

TWO ADVERTISEMENTS FOR THE SALE OF THE WHEATSHEAF

© *Picture copyright and courtesy of Berrow's Worcester Journal*

Berrow's Worcester Journal, 7th February 1788, p.1

𝕿𝖔 𝕭𝖊 𝕾𝖔𝖑𝖉 𝕭𝖞 𝕻𝖗𝖎𝖛𝖆𝖙𝖊 𝕮𝖔𝖓𝖙𝖗𝖆𝖈𝖙

All that copyhold messuage or tenement, with stables, outbuildings and garden thereto belonging, known by the name of The Wheatsheaf, situate in Bewdley in the county of Worcester, and now let to Mr. David Rowland, at the yearly rent of £24...

n.b. The £24 rent does not match the total Annual Rental of 14s-6d. (72.5p) for numbers 21-23 which was quoted both in the Manor Court Rolls of 19th century and when the property was enfranchised in 1902.

Poster [23]

Well-Established Inn, Bewdley

1805 a Well-Established Inn, Bewdley, to be sold by Auction by W. Handy on Monday 4th March next on the premises between the hours of 4pm and 6pm

All that well-established Inn, known by the name of the **WHEAT SHEAF**, desirably situated in the Centre of the market-place in the borough of Bewdley, now and for some years past in the Occupation of Mr. Benjamin Giles; consisting of a good Dwelling-house, with a spacious Yard, Commodious Stabling and convenient Offices, The whole in good repair and may be entered upon at Midsummer next.

The Copyhold Held by the Manor of Bewdley, a tenure little inferior to Freehold, and the Land Tax redeemed.

Chapter Two

COACHING

Although vehicles such as chariots had long been used by richer people in this country,[24] the *coach* was not introduced into Britain until the sixteenth century.[25] One tradition relates that the first coach built in England was for the Earl of Rutland in *c*1554. Certainly, historians accept that, by 1564, Queen Elizabeth I owned one, probably made in Holland. It is said that, despite preferring to ride on horse-back "she was not averse to parading in her plume-capped, curtained coach … even at the risk of 'coaching pains from being knocked about'."[26]

The first stagecoaches appeared in Britain in the early 16th century[27] but, apparently, it was not until about 1800 that 'ordinary' people in England started to become used to riding in public coaches.[28] Small wonder, perhaps. Not only was it expensive, but also uncomfortable and dangerous.

Before the advent of the General Turnpike Act in 1773 minor roads were usually little more than narrow tracks, miry or flooded in winter and with hard, dry ruts in summer. 'Main' roads – the King's Highway – although wider, to allow two wagons to pass, suffered from similar problems.[29] Even when materials were used to form a firmer basis, road surfaces were still distinctly uneven and there were many accidents. Add to these conditions the hazards of obstacles left in the road, highwaymen and footpads,[30] no street lighting and the long stretches of isolated track, and one can imagine that travelling on these swaying vehicles was positively stressful.

Passengers would have had to rely on the coachman's sobriety as well as on his skill in ensuring that his horses were well-matched in both strength and temperament. The horses must have been exhausted quite quickly, not only by the hazardous road surfaces, but also by the weights they had to pull.

The coaches themselves must have been rather cramped and either hot or cold – inside as well as outside – according to the season. One hopes that travelling companions were compatible.[31]

Improvements were gradually made in the construction of coaches and of roads and the early 19th century saw the establishment of a regular service of stagecoaches between the towns and villages of Great Britain.

Usually, each proprietor had not one but *several* coaches of the same name.[32] Drawn by four horses[33] – five or six in steep places[34] – which were exchanged frequently at staging posts along the route, the stagecoaches ran to strict timetables, an average speed seemingly being about 10 miles per hour.[35]

By mid-19th century, passengers had a choice of transport: *mail coaches* – the fastest vehicles – carried four passengers inside and six outside; *stagecoaches* – slightly slower – could carry up to eighteen passengers; *postcoaches* – used by wealthier travellers and hired from inns which specialised in doing so.[36]

Doubtless, stories of those days abound. Locally, many were the tales told of the **Red Rover** which called at Bewdley's **Wheatsheaf** en route for Birmingham/Ludlow from *c*1840 to *c*1850. Reputed to have acquired its name because the coachman grew increasingly "red-faced and reckless" as he imbibed rum and milk at the different stops, the title could equally have derived from the fact that a wheel was often set on fire by sparks engendered by friction of wood against stone as the coach dashed over the cobblestones. For that reason, the coach always carried a spare.[37] One wonders whether the passengers considered the fares paid worth the risk to life and limb.

The metal tracks which can still be seen in the entry to today's Bewdley Institute – although not in the original entry to the inn – are said to have been used by coaches calling at the *Wheatsheaf* to protect the access from damage by the vehicles' wheels. The narrower the wheels, the more damage they did to the road surface – hence vehicles with narrow wheels rated a higher toll than that charged for vehicles with broad wheels.[38]

Isaac Wedley, writing in *c*1914, quotes from a table of tolls painted on a large board (once) fastened against the turnpike cottage in Welch Gate: "for every coach, sociable, chariot, Berlin, landau, vis-à-vis, curricle, calash, whiskey, tax cart, hearse or litter, 6d. (2.5p) shall be paid. For any timber wagon, or vehicle with wheels less than six inches (153mm) wide, 7d. (just under 3p): if more than six inches 4d. (just over 1.5p)." He noted that costs were doubled between October and April. Perhaps this was because, as already noted, during the winter months the roads were likely to be muddier and therefore more easily damaged than in the drier summer months.

All was not gloom, however. By 1830 there was little danger from robbery. Guards, originally employed as a deterrent to highwaymen, etc., travelled on most long-distance stage- and mailcoaches. Among his many duties, the *guard* looked after the passengers and was usually a far more entertaining travelling companion than the *coachman*.[39] There was, however, at least one jolly exception to this locally in the person of Mr. Jordan, coachman of **L' Hirondelle**, which ran between Cheltenham and Liverpool via Kidderminster: "He would sometimes, in coming down Hagley Hill, lasso a duck at the *Fountain,* landing it on the lap of the passenger on the box seat. At the *Swan Inn* he would place a half-dozen tumblers on the dining table and neatly take out the spoons without upsetting the glasses."[40]

Both the coachman, who was "king",[41] and the guard were rather splendidly dressed fellows and the stagecoaches very colourful – in contrast to the elegant Royal Mail coaches, which were "painted in the royal livery of scarlet, maroon and black, with the imperial arms emblazoned in gold on their door panels."[42]

Once in the town the guard would sound his horn[43] continually until he reached the inn to warn the innkeeper of his vehicle's approach.[44] One can readily imagine the excitement of the crowds who would gather to watch their arrival and departure.

In Kidderminster, an attractive annual custom on 1st May saw the horses of each coach given new harness and decorated with flowers, while the coachmen and guards received "new coats and hats and the guardsmen enlivened the occasion with music from their cornets".[45]

In general, the insides of the coaching inns seem to have been comfortable and welcoming and to have provided a variety of wholesome food.[46] Customers might have had the newspapers read to them by a reader, for Broadfield,[47] writing in *c*1889, tells of an ancient custom which "was discontinued about 50 years ago. ... the reader was thought a deal of in those days; he had his refreshments free, and read from the papers about an hour upon any subject called for by the company – politics, trade, war, &c. Many persons at that time could not read, and public information was thus obtained in a quiet, pleasant manner. One reader (a tailor) who generally read to a company of tailors admitted that whenever he came to a hard word he always said "Sleeveboard." At the close of the reading the company indulged in discussion."

Wedley[48] relates that, in the early 19th century, the only newspaper which got through to Wribbenhall – *The London Standard* – belonged to a local lawyer. He allowed the parish clerk to read it to customers in the parlour of the *Black Boy* on Thursday nights.

MR. THOMAS COOPER,
THE READER AT THE "PLOUGH."
(Copied exact from a Water-color drawing.)

Ye OLDE Reader 1751.

ДHW 1886.

The Reader at the Plough, Kidderminster.
Reproduced from Edward Broadfield's Guide to Kidderminster & Neighbourhood.
Printed by W. Hepworth, 1889.

It seems, however, that at least one local coach was usually quicker to bring the news to Bewdley than did either the newspapers or the post. According to Mrs. Parker, it was Bewdley coachman John Lewis's proud boast that he brought the news of Waterloo to the town only about 10 days after the Battle had been won. One likes to imagine his horses hastening along, adorned with flowers or ribbons in celebration.[49]

Some Press Cuttings about Highwaymen, Road Conditions, etc.

18th August 1774[50]

"On Thursday evening, about 8 o'clock, Dr. Ingram, coming in a post chaise from Kew to London, was stopped by a single highwayman near Gunnersbury Lane, who robbed him of his purse, containing about three guineas (£3.15) and some silver; but the man politely returned his watch, and desired him if he was stopped again, to give the words, "High for the Sod". The Doctor was soon after attacked by another highwayman, near the Fo(u)r-mile Post, Hammersmith, and on acting according to his instructions, the fellow rode off, wishing him a "Goodnight"."

Berrow's Worcester Journal, 22nd January 1789, p.3

"Last week was committed to Hereford gaol, by John Glasse, clerk, one Francis Crump, a waterman, belonging to the town of Bewdley; charged on the oath of John Dawson, of Bromyard, with stopping him on the King's Highway, between Leominster and Bromyard, in company with another man, not yet taken, who stood by him with a bludgeon, while Crump rifled his pocket." © *Picture copyright and courtesy of Berrow's Worcester Journal.*

25th June 1789[51]

"In consequence of Ascot races, Mr. Skey, junior of Bewdley, in this county, and two ladies could (not), on Wednesday evening, be accommodated at Salt Hill with beds, where they arrived about nine o'clock, and being similarly disappointed at Maidenhead Bridge, they were consequently under the necessity of proceeding to Henley, and in the long lane leading to Maidenhead thicket, they were suddenly attacked by two footpads, armed with cutlasses and pistols, who after compelling the driver to stop, the two (one on each side the chaise) broke all the windows with their pistols; and with horrid imprecations demanded purses, watches, etc. Mr. S. lost his watch, purse, and many other trifles, in his pockets, (which the villains had the audacity to search). One of the ladies lost her watch and purse, and the other her purse and pocket book; but an immediate and particular description of the different articles were sent to the public offices in London, 'tis hoped it will lead to a discovery. The purses only contain about ten guineas (£10.50)."

Berrow's Worcester Journal, 8th October 1795, p.3

"Monday night last, as the Bewdley postman was riding on the road near Ombersley, it being very dark, the horse fell over a load of gravel which had been left in the middle of the highway, and threw his rider some distance; fortunately, however, neither man nor horse received any material injury. A gentleman, attended by his servants, coming to this city (Worcester), very narrowly escaped the same fate. We mention this circumstance merely as a hint to the surveyors, with the hope that they will order workmen in future, not to leave impediments in the middle of the roads to endanger the lives of passengers whose business obliges them to be out after dark." © *Picture copyright and courtesy of Berrow's Worcester Journal.*

Berrow's Worcester Journal, 12th December 1799, p.3

"Early on Saturday morning last, the post-boy conveying mail from this City to Bewdley, was stopped on the road about two miles from hence by a single footpad, and robbed of the Bewdley, Kidderminster, Stourbridge, and Stourport bags. The boy immediately returned back to this city and gave information of the robbery. – Three of the bags were found in the course of the day in a ditch on Bevere Green, one of which had been opened, but it did not appear that anything had been taken out." © *Picture copyright and courtesy of Berrow's Worcester Journal.*

Worcestershire Guardian, 25th July 1835, p.8

"Yesterday evening, between six and seven o'clock, (there was) a very serious accident in Bewdley to a coach purporting to be the the 'Owen Glendower' (although the one used was an old one called 'The Emerald') on its route from Aberystwyth to Birmingham. As the coach was crossing Bewdley Bridge, the horses gave a sudden jerk at the turn on the Wribbenhall side, when the bolt which connects the body of the coach with the fore wheels gave way, and the vehicle was overturned with a tremendous crash. There were no fewer than <u>seventeen</u> passengers inside and out, in addition to the coachman and guard. Though several of the passengers were much hurt, most providentially no life was lost; Mr. H. Hill of Rock, Mr. Morris of Leominster (a proprietor) and some passengers from Aberystwyth received the most serious injuries, and some of them were obliged to remain at Bewdley. Dr. Davis of Presteign (sic) (who was on his route to Oxford to attend the meeting of the Midland Medical Association), Mr. Phillips of the same place, Mr. Taylor of Oldswinford, Mr., Mrs. and Miss Hughes of Dudley and others were enabled to pursue their journey.

The inside passengers (Mrs. and Miss Acton of Birmingham, Mr. Chinner of Dudley and Mrs. Taylor of Oldswinford) were not in the least hurt. The inhabitants of Bewdley and Wribbenhall manifested the utmost sympathy for the sufferers by the accident, and rendered them all the aid that kindness could suggest. When the coach was upset, the horses broke away with the pole and two wheels; they were headed in trying to make the turn to Kidderminster, and wheeling round suddenly they (some of them probably being blind) were precipitated off the quay into the Severn, a fall of at least 15 feet (approx. 4.62 metres). One valuable mare belonging to Messrs. Godfrey of Kidderminster was killed, but others were extricated by the gallant exertions of some watermen who, at great peril, cut the harness and got them out of the river. It appears that a defect in the bolt was observed at Leominster, and the coach was detained there some time to repair it. The proprietors are much to blame in running an old coach, and in suffering it to be overloaded."

Although not a local story, the biter was bitten in the following episode:[52]

Towards the end of 1718 the stagecoach from Colchester to London was stopped by a highwayman. The coachman having forewarned his lone passenger that he had seen the highwayman approaching, the eminent lady "acted the part of a madwoman naturally". She hurriedly removed her lace cap and pulled her hair into a wild mess before he arrived. When he pointed his pistol at her, she leapt out of the coach door and grasped one of the highwayman's legs, shrieking piteously that she was so glad to meet her cousin Tom and begging him to rescue her from "the rogue of a coachman who was taking her by that rogue of (her) husband's orders to Bedlam, for a mad woman". The highwayman, not surprisingly, vehemently denied being the lady's cousin and added that Bedlam was the best place for her. The coachman confirmed that he was taking the lady to Bedlam on her husband's orders. "E'en take her then," replied the highwayman, one Nicholas Horner, "for thinking to have met with a good bait, I find now there's nothing to be had of this mad toad". Thereupon he "set spurs to his horse as fast as he could, for fear he should be plagued with her, for she seemed mighty fond of her cousin, whom she ran after a good way; but after he was gone clean off, she was more pleased with his absence than his sight, and got safe to London."

Footnote: *Nicholas Horner was caught after a later robbery and hanged on 3rd April 1719, aged 32.*

Illustration of what is believed to have been the Signboard from the former Highwayman Café in Stourport Road, Bewdley by local artist Sydney H. Jones, c1950s. All efforts have been taken to identify the copyright owner/s without success. I apologize for any infringement and invite copyright owners to make contact with me.

Chapter Three

COACHING IN BEWDLEY BEFORE 1835

Coaching is thought to have begun in Bewdley after 1760.[53] One of the first coaches traced in the town so far is the ***Ludlow Flying stage-coach*** which, in **1762**, called at the *Saracen's Head*[54] twice per week, thence to London via the *Golden Lion*, Kidderminster.[55]

On Tuesday, 31st March **1778 *the Bewdley and Birmingham Diligence*** left the *George*, Load Street at 10.00am for Birmingham and returned on Wednesday, 1st April at 2.00pm, "to continue going every Tuesday and Wednesday throughout the year."[56]

A press cutting of April **1782**[57] records a ***Bewdley and London Diligence*** leaving the *George* on Mondays, Wednesdays and Fridays to arrive at the *Bull and Mouth* in the capital on the following day, while the reverse journey was timetabled to leave London for Bewdley on the same three days. "Fare one guinea (£1.05). Children on lap half price. Fourteen pounds luggage allowed, all above, one penny per pound (approx. 0.42p for about 450g)."

The Flying Wagons in the following advertisement seem to have been of two types – one for passengers[58] and one for goods: In June **1784**, "Hereford, Leominster, Ledbury, Bewdley, Kidderminster and Worcester **FLYING WAGONS**, upon an entirely new construction from London to Worcester in thirty hours. Set out from *Cross Keys Inn*, Wood Street, Cheapside, and the *Saracen's Head Inn*, every Sunday, Tuesday, Thursday evenings, at 7 o'clock, and return every Monday, Wednesday and Friday evenings, to London. The above **coaches and wagons** call at the *Old White Horse* cellar, Piccadilly, going out and coming in to London… The proprietors of the above undertaking flatter themselves that the above wagons will be of the greatest utility to the public in general, as the carriage is invented to convey the goods, though in so short a time, as safe, swift, and easy as in any coach."[59]

Also **at some time between *c*1777 and *c*1813** a ***Bewdley Diligence*** set off from the *George Inn* every Saturday morning at 8 o'clock for Worcester, leaving there at 4.00pm for Bewdley – return fare 6s-0d. (30p), single fare 4s-0d. (20p).[60]

The Prattinton Collections[61] include a press cutting of (December) **1782** which reads:

"GEORGE INN BEWDLEY 1782
A BEWDLEY AND BRISTOL COACH,

Through Worcester, Upton, Tewkesbury, and Gloucester,
Will begin on Wednesday next, and continue going
Every Wednesday and Saturday morning, at five o'clock,
And arrive at the Greyhound Inn in Bristol the same Evening.
Performed under the Direction of
The Public and obedient humble Servants,
J. CRUMP, Bewdley   J. PAINE, Gloucester
T. HUXLEY, Worcester   T. POSTIN, Bristol."

Another source of the same date[62] adds:

"Also, a coach will set out from the above inn, in Bristol on Wednesday and Saturday morning, at 2 o'clock, and arrive at Bewdley early the same evening...

Fare:		
	From Bewdley to Worcester	3s-6d. (17.5p)
	From Bewdley to Upton	6s-0d. (30p)
	From Bewdley to Tewkesbury	7s-0d. (35p)
	From Bewdley to Gloucester	9s-6d. (47.5p)
	From Bewdley to Bristol	16s-0d. (80p)
	Outsides, half fare – short passengers,	3d. (1.25p) per mile."

"UNICORN INN. The only **Bath, Bristol, and Hollyhead** POST COACH that travels the new road through North Wales, and avoids the very dangerous ferry at Conway" is reported in March **1787**.[63] The press cutting continues: "A new and elegant post coach, will set out from the White Lion in the Market place, Bath, on Monday the 12th of February instant, at 4 o'clock, and from the Bush Tavern, Corn Street, Bristol at 6 o'clock in the morning, for Hollyhead, by way of Gloucester, Tewkesbury, Worcester, Bewdley, Bridgnorth and Shrewsbury; and will continue to run every Monday, Wednesday, and Friday at the same hour. The proprietors respectfully inform those ladies and gentlemen who shall chuse (sic) to travel in this coach that it will stop all night at the Unicorn in Worcester, the

Lion in Shrewsbury, and the Bull in Conway, at which place the coach will arrive early on each evening, and they may rest assured that every exertion will be made to render their journey as agreeable and convenient as possible. Fare: Inside to Shrewsbury £1-12s-0d. (£1.60) Hollyhead £3-14s-0d. (£3.70)

Performed by:

ARNOLD, Bath	SALISBURY & DAVIS, Oswestry
WEEKS & CO., Bristol	PARKER & EDWARDS, Llangollen
JONES & HINKS, Gloucester	HARRIS, Corwen
WILLIAMS, Worcester	ROWLANDS, Fernidge Manor
CRUMP, Bewdley (the *George*)	READ & HOUSE, Conway
CORBET, Bridgnorth	JACKSON, Bangor Ferry
LAWRENCE, Shrewsbury	JACKSON, Hollyhead."

In **1794** the ***Bewdley, Kidderminster and Birmingham Post Coach*** set out from the *George* at 6.00am every Monday and Thursday and returned from Birmingham for Bewdley at 2.00pm.[64]

The Bewdley section of Lewis's **1820** Directory, under *Land and Water Carriage*, cites: "**MAIL**, to Worcester every Afternoon; to Kidderminster, Stourbridge, and Dudley, every Morning; **SMITH'S CARAVAN**, to Worcester Monday, Wednesday, and Saturday Mornings."

In the *Evesham Journal*, 12th and 19th September 1931, p.11 of each, Mr. E. A. B. Barnard notes **"Some Bewdley Stage-coaches, 1823-1829"**, from Peter Prattinton's Collections:

"in January **1823**, the ***New Royal Mail*** left the *George*, Bewdley daily at 1.15, arriving at the *Swan with two Necks*, Lad Lane, London at 7 o'clock the following morning. It returned therefrom each evening at 7.30pm (7.00pm on Sundays), to arrive in Bewdley at 12.30 the next day. The journey went via Kidderminster, Stourbridge, Dudley and Birmingham."

"Cheap Travelling, by the Only Direct Route to Ludlow" appeared in an undated advertisement, but probably for **1824**, when the ***Greyhound*** ran from the *Swan Hotel*, Birmingham on Mondays, Wednesdays and Fridays at 8.30am and arrived at the *Feathers Inn* by 5.00pm "Route: Dudley, Stourbridge, Kidderminster, Bewdley and Cleobury Mortimer. Fare: Inside to Ludlow, 12s-0d. (60p); Outside, 7s-0d. (35p)."

Perhaps as an added incentive, the notice continued: *"N.B. – The same Coach and Coachman throughout. Performed by the Public's obedient Servants, Thomas Waddell*[65] *& Co."*

A venture which failed after only a short time was Mark Nutting's **Accommodation**, "a Light and Easy Coach" which, in **May 1827**, left the *Black Boy Inn*, Wribbenhall, on Mondays, Wednesdays and Saturdays at 7.00am for Worcester, where it arrived "in time to meet Coaches to Cheltenham, Gloucester, Bath, Bristol, Malvern, Hereford, Hay, Leominster and Ludlow, and return(ed) from thence at quarter past 4 o'clock in the Afternoon, from the Currier's Arms, Angel Street, and will call at the Hop-Market Inn; Fare: Outside, 2s-6d. (12.5p); Inside 4s-6d. (22.5p)."

Perhaps due to stiff competition, the service was not as successful as he had hoped, so Mr. Nutting reduced the fares, "Outside, 2s-0d. (10p); Inside 3s-6d. (17.5p)" and altered the route slightly to leave Bewdley's *George* for Worcester's *Hop Pole Inn* – but to no avail.

THE ROYAL SOVEREIGN DAY COACH.

W. & J. LEWIS,

Beg most respectfully to return their sincere thanks to their Friends and the Public in general, for the liberal Patronage they have received since running the above Coach, and beg to inform them they continue doing so from the George Inn, Bewdley, every Morning (Sunday excepted) at 7 o'clock precisely, calls at the Black Star Stourport, and arrives at the Star & Garter Hotel, Worcester, at a ¼ past 9, in time for the first London, Bath, Bristol, Cheltenham, Gloucester, Ludlow, Hereford and Bromyard Coaches, and returns in the Evening, at 5 o'clock.

Parcels, Packages, &c., punctually Delivered and Forwarded to any Part of the Kingdom, upon as reasonable Terms as any other conveyance upon the Road.

Bewdley, May 22nd, 1827. —— [DANKS TYP.]

W. & J. Lewis's Trade Card for the Royal Sovereign Day Coach from Peter Prattinton's Collections for a History of Worcestershire. Reproduced by kind permission of The Society of Antiquaries, London.

1784 illustration of the First Mail Coach. © The British Postal Museum &
Archive, London, and reproduced by their kind permission.

In **May 1827** W. & J. Lewis thanked their customers "for the liberal
Patronage" they had received since running the ***Royal Sovereign Day Coach***,
and informed them that the coach would continue to leave the *George Inn*,
Bewdley, at 7.00am daily, except Sunday, via Stourport, the *Black Star*, en
route for Worcester, the *Star and Garter Hotel*, where it would arrive at
9.15am "in time for the first London, Bath, Bristol, Cheltenham,
Gloucester, Ludlow, Hereford and Bromyard Coaches, and (would return)
in the Evening at 5 o'clock. Parcels, Packages, etc., punctually Delivered
and Forwarded to any Part of the Kingdom, upon as reasonable Terms as
any other conveyance upon the Road. Bewdley, May 22nd, 1827."

20th **October 1829** saw a new coach service advertised: "*WHEATSHEAF
INN* AND POST OFFICE, BEWDLEY. The Public are respectfully informed,
a New Coach, called ***The Greyhound***, has commenced running, and will

continue to leave the above Inn every afternoon, at half-past Two o'clock, to the Swan and Albion Inns, Birmingham, in time for the coaches to London, which will arrive by Eight o'clock the following morning; and by which places may be secured at the above Inn. The Mail will continue as usual.

Inside to Birmingham, 5s. (25p); Outside 2s-6d. (12.5p)

Inside to London, £2 (£2.00); Outside £1-1s (£1.05)

Small Parcels, 1s-8d. (just over 8p) each. Luggage, ½d. (about 0.21p) per lb. (approx. 450g). Performed by the Public's obedient Servants, H. Godfrey and Co.[66] Oct. 20, 1829".

Although local service the **Emerald** evidently did not go through Bewdley in **1829**, one of the partners who ran it was **Thomas Ree** who may have been the same Thomas Ree who ran the *Sovereign* in 1823 and a one-time resident at Bewdley's *George Inn*. (see p.25). The other partner was Charles Badenhurst[67] & Co. The **Emerald**[68] went from the *Crown Inn*, Stourbridge – daily, at 4.30pm – to the *Nelson Hotel*, Birmingham, where it arrived "in time for that favourite conveyance, the **Emerald Night Coach**, through Coventry and St. Albans, to the *Cross Keys*, Wood Street, Cheapside, and *Golden Cross*, Charing Cross, London."

Chapter Four

THE HEYDAY OF COACHING
AT THE WHEATSHEAF

T he heyday of coaching at the *Wheatsheaf* seems to have been from *c*1835 to *c*1850 and, during that time, the *Wheatsheaf* and the *George* are said to have vied with each other for supremacy.

In addition to the services listed below, there were probably feeder services between Bewdley and e.g. Kidderminster.[69]

In **1835** Pigot's Directory records *at least three coaches* serving Bewdley, *two* of which called at the **Wheatsheaf:**

*"***To Birmingham:** *the* **Royal Mail** *(from Stourport) calling daily at the* **Wheatsheaf** *at 3.00pm"* just half an hour before *"letters for London, etc.",* were *"despatched daily at 3.30pm from the Post Office, (probably today's number 14) Load Street"*; <u>and</u>:

"the **Union** *(from Ludlow) calling daily at the Wheatsheaf at 2.00pm."* Both went via Kidderminster, Stourbridge and Dudley.

*"***To Ludlow** *(via Cleobury): the* **Union** *(from Birmingham) daily, leaving the* **Wheatsheaf** *at 1.00pm."*

*"***To Stourport:** *the* **Royal Mail** *(from Birmingham) calling every day at the* **Wheatsheaf** *at 11.00am"* the very time at which *"Letters from London, etc., arrive every forenoon at the Post Office, Load Street."*

*"***To Worcester:** *the* **Sovereign***, from the* **George Inn** *every morning (Sunday excepted) at seven; goes thro' Stourport and Ombersley."*

Kenneth Hobson[70] adds a fourth, as well as referring to various other Bewdley coach services for other years:

"In **1835**

    To Birmingham: *The **British Queen Omnibus** calls at the **George** every morning at 7.15."*

He also includes (in 1835):

    "***To Birmingham:*** *The **Royal Mail** (from Ludlow) calls at the **George** every evening at 7.15.*

    To Ludlow: *The **Royal Mail** (via Cleobury Mortimer) (from the **George**) every morning at 6.30."*

The ***Sovereign*** – also advertised in 1827, above – was (still) run by ***local coach proprietor* John Lewis** in **1835**. There appear to have been two local coach proprietors of the same name: John Lewis (senior) could have been about 13 or 23 years older than John Lewis (junior).

John (junior) was born in Bewdley in *c*1804. Not mentioned in the Bewdley/Wribbenhall section of Pigot's 1835 Directory, nor in that section of Billing's Directory for 1855, he was listed as "Coach Proprietor, *Wribbenhall*" in **1840**.[71] The **1851** Census records him at *Severn Side*, aged 47, married to Caroline (aged 36, born in Cleobury Mortimer) and having 2 daughters (Sarah, aged 19 and Ellen, 9) and a son (John, aged 11) – all 3 born in Bewdley. Perhaps he was the *"J. Lewis"* recorded in Bates' Directory of stage coach services 1836[72] as "licenced, (number 7517, to carry 4 passengers inside and 8 outside, 1 single journey, Monday to Saturday) *Worcester and Bewdley.*" His licence number, allocated by the Commissioners for the Affairs of Stamps, would have been displayed on a plate on the coach.[73]

Or maybe John Lewis (senior) was the proprietor. Mrs. Parker[74] recalls: "W. & J. Lewis were the sons of the gatekeeper on Bewdley Bridge and formerly on Gloucester Bridge. John was born in 1791 (c1781?) and died in 1893 (1882?[75]). They drove the Worcester coach. John's was the last coach to run from Worcester after the opening of the Severn Valley Line to Shrewsbury."[76]

Evidently, the ***Sovereign*** was also the *first* coach to run between Bewdley and Worcester. The *Ten Towns Messenger* of 2nd February 1849 reports, under *Deaths:* "January 25th, at his late residence, the Old Hall Farm, parish of Rock, Worcestershire, Mr. Thomas Ree[77], in the 73rd year of his age. He was an enterprising man, and formerly lived at the George Hotel, Bewdley, and established the first coach to run between Bewdley and

Worcester on the 14th of June, 1823, and is continued by Mr. John Lewis to the present day."

Perhaps it was this same Thomas Ree who, in 1829, together with a partner, ran the *Emerald Coach* from Stourbridge to Birmingham. (see p.23).

In **1836** the ***Royal Mail*** coach may have been operated by **James Hearn & Co.**, one of the principal proprietors of long-distance stage- and mailcoaches from and to London at that time.[78] The timetable was as follows, times of the return journey being given in brackets:

London, Kings Arms, Snow Hill	7.30pm	(7.11am)
(a principal coaching establishment)		
General Post Office, London	8.00pm	(6.56am)
Aylesbury	12.15am	(2.41am)
Bicester	1.57am	(12.59am)
Banbury	3.30am	(11.26pm)
Southam	4.55am	(10.01pm)
Warwick	5.52am	(9.04pm)
Birmingham	7.56am	(7.00pm)
Birmingham	8.15am	(6.40pm)
Kidderminster	10.22am	(4.24pm)
Stourport	11.03am	(3.43pm)

Bates[79] records cross-country and local Royal Mail Coaches which included services: departing from Birmingham at 8.00am for Stourport, returning from there at 3.15pm and departing from Birmingham at 7.45am for Worcester, returning from there at 3.00pm.

Interestingly, the same source cites **J. Barnett**[80] running a coach service between <u>Birmingham and Bewdley</u>, "Licence number 7524, to carry 9 passengers inside (none mentioned outside) 1 return journey Monday/Tuesday, Thursday/Friday." No further details are given.

Bentley's Directory of **1840** records *five* coaches serving the town, *three* of which called at the ***Wheatsheaf:***

*"**To Birmingham:** the **Royal Mail** (from Ludlow) calls at the **Wheatsheaf** every evening at 7 o'clock"; only 15 minutes before "Letters from Ludlow, Tenbury, S. Wales, etc. arrive every evening at the Post Office, High Street (sic)" & "Letters to London, Birmingham, Dudley, Kidderminster, Stourbridge and all parts N., E. and S. are despatched"* from there; <u>and</u>

*"the **Red Rover** leaves the **Wheatsheaf** daily at 11.30am, fare 5s (25p) outside and 8s (40p) inside."* Both went via Kidderminster, Stourbridge and Dudley; <u>and</u>

*"the **Emperor** (from Stourport) calls at the **Wheatsheaf** every morning at 7.30, fare 3s-6d. (17.5p) outside and 4s (20p) inside. Goes via Kidderminster and Halesowen";* <u>and</u>

*"the **Favourite**, leaves the **Waggon and Horses**, Welch Gate, every Monday and Thursday at 9.00am."*

*"**To Ludlow** (via Cleobury Mortimer): the **Royal Mail** (from Birmingham) calls at the **Wheatsheaf** every morning at 6.20"* just 5 minutes before *"Letters to Ludlow, Tenbury, S. Wales, etc. are despatched by mail every morning from the Post Office, High Street"* & *"Letters from London, Birmingham, Dudley, Kidderminster, Stourbridge and all parts N. and S. arrive every morning"* there; <u>and</u>

*(via Tenbury and Leominster) "the **Red Rover**, calling at the **Wheatsheaf** daily at 5.00pm, fare 6s (30p) outside and 10s (50p) inside."*

*"**To Worcester**: the **Sovereign**, from the **George Inn**, daily at 8.15am, fare 3s (15p) inside and 5s (25p) outside"* (sic). It was usually more expensive to travel inside than out, so perhaps these amounts have been transposed – or perhaps 3s is a misprint for 8s (40p).

In **1842** Pigot's Directory records *three* coaches and *three* omnibuses serving Bewdley, *one* coach and *one* omnibus calling at the **Wheatsheaf**.

*"**To Birmingham: the Royal Mail** (from Ludlow) calls at the **George** every evening at 7.15"* at the same time as *"Letters are despatched to London, etc. every evening from the Post Office, Load Street";* <u>and</u>

the *"**Red Rover** (from Ludlow) calls at the **Wheat Sheaf** (sic) every forenoon at 11.00";* <u>and</u>

*"the **British Queen Omnibus** calls at the **George** every morning at 7.15; (all go through Kidderminster, Stourbridge, Dudley, West Bromwich, etc.)";* <u>and</u>

*"the **Emperor Omnibus** from the **Wheat Sheaf** every morning at 7.00 (goes through Kidderminster, Hagley, Hales Owen (sic), etc.)";* <u>and</u>

*"the **Favourite Omnibus** from the **Waggon & Horses** every Monday and Tuesday morning at 9.00 (goes the same route)."*

*"**To Ludlow** (via Cleobury Mortimer): the **Royal Mail** (from Birmingham) calls at the **George** every morning at 6.30"* just half an hour after *"Letters from London, etc. arrive every morning at the Post Office, Load Street";* <u>and</u>

*"the **Red Rover** from the **Wheat Sheaf** every afternoon at 5.00 (goes through Tenbury and Leominster)."*

*"**To Worcester:** the **Sovereign** from the **George Inn** every morning (except Sunday) at 8.30 (goes through Stourport and Ombersley)."*

Slater's Directory for **1850** named *three* coaches and *one* omnibus which came through Bewdley, all of which called at the **Wheatsheaf**, *except the Royal Mail on its way to Ludlow* – see below:

*"**To Birmingham:** the **Royal Mail** (from Ludlow) calls at the **George** and at the **Wheatsheaf** daily at 12 (noon)";* <u>and</u>

*"the **Red Rover** (from Ludlow) calls at the **Wheatsheaf** daily at 11.30am."* Both went via Kidderminster, Stourbridge, Dudley and West Bromwich; <u>and</u>

*"the **Victoria Omnibus**, from **Gardeners Office**,*[81] *Load Street, every morning at twenty minutes before seven, calling at the **George Hotel** and **Wheatsheaf**; goes through Kidderminster, Hagley, Halesowen, &c."*

*"**To Ludlow** (via Cleobury Mortimer): the **Royal Mail** (from Birmingham) calls at the **George Hotel**, daily at 5.55am"* – but not at the Wheatsheaf, it seems – a quarter of an hour after *"Letters from London and various places arrive – from Birmingham – every morning at the Post Office, Load Street";* <u>and</u>

*"(via Tenbury and Leominster) the **Red Rover**, from the **Wheatsheaf** daily at 5.30pm."*

*"**To Worcester** (via Stourport and Ombersley): the **Sovereign**, from the **Wheatsheaf** daily at 7.30am."*

Five years later, in **1855**,[82] however, there is no mention of coaches or omnibuses. **Ann Allcott** – victualler at the **Wheatsheaf** – was merely "licensed to let horses[83] and gigs", whereas the *George* was described as "a family and commercial hotel and posting house", while the name of the licensee, **John Parsons**, also appeared under "Horse and gig letters".

In **1862**[84] the *Wheatsheaf* and the *George* were still the only two inns recorded in Bewdley. The latter was "a commercial and posting house" and the licensee, **John Parsons**, was a "horse, gig, etc." owner who ran an omnibus from his inn twice daily to Kidderminster.

Ann Allcott was still the licensee at the *Wheatsheaf* in **1862**, but she no longer appears to have been licensed to let horses[85] and gigs. Perhaps there was not enough business for two such operators once the Railway had opened in Bewdley.

James Hinton operated a *carrier* service from the *Wheatsheaf* to Ludlow on Thursdays and Saturdays in **1862**. Such a service had been run twice a week from the *George* to Birmingham/Kidderminster as far back as *c*1840-*c*1850 and there were also other carrier services being run in the town during that time, but not from the *Wheatsheaf*.

In **1873** an *omnibus* still ran from the *George*, but only as far as Bewdley Railway Station, where it "attend(ed) the arrival and departure of all trains".[86] Although the service from the *George* to the Railway Station continued until about 1896,[87] **by 1873** both the *omnibus* to Kidderminster and the *carrier* service ran from the ***Dog Wheel Inn***, Dog Lane. The *carrier* service was operated by **Benjamin Breakwell and W. Jones** and the *omnibus* by **Edward Plevey**, who lived on the premises.

Interestingly, in **1891**[88] Bewdley-born **Edward Plevey** was an *Innkeeper & Cab Proprietor* in Dog Lane,[89] married, aged 49, while his son Edward, aged 17 and also born in Bewdley, although employed as a *coach builder*, might not have worked for his father.[90]

The advent of railways, 1825-1840's, heralded the end of the coaching era nationally. Initially, it seems to have been the general belief that railways would be used merely for carrying freight, leaving coaches for passengers – clearly seen as advantageous all round. Besides, it was thought that travel by rail was too dangerous to attract passengers. By the 1830s, however, it was plain that railways posed a serious challenge to coaching.[91] The carrying and river[92] trades and the canals must also have been wary of competition from the railways.

Maybe the proprietors of coaching inns, through their wide range of contacts, were in a better position than most to learn of the potential threat to their livelihood which this new form of transport represented.

In Bewdley, the decline in business apparently began even as coaching appeared to reach its zenith in *c*1836, although the Act to build the line along the Severn Valley was not passed until 1853.[93] The previous year, on 1st May, the railway had opened in Kidderminster,[94] approximately 3 miles (about 4.8 kilometres) north-east of Bewdley. Instrumental in its establishment was Lord Ward of Dudley,[95] Lord of the Manor of Wribbenhall since 1838,[96] whose family were lessees of the Manor of Bewdley after 1841 until 1870[97] and owners of Witley Court from 1837-1920.[98]

Among other people having local associations and first-hand knowledge or experience of railways were **Joseph Sturge**, a former resident and cornfactor in Bewdley who had been chosen as one of the first Directors of the London and Birmingham Railway Company before 1836;[99] and **Joseph Tangye**, the Birmingham entrepreneur who was to purchase Tickenhill in *c*1873 and who had known the Sturge family for many years.[100] Joseph and his brother, James, had worked under Brunel for Mr. Brunton, engineer to the West Cornwall Railway before *c*1852.[101]

Yet their expertise had not made them unmindful of the disruption wrought in people's lives and in the landscape by the railways, and they were only too well aware of some other disadvantages. Mr. Tangye's daughter, Mrs. Alice Parker, *c*1873-1960,[102] wrote[103] that the railways – although greatly desired by the rapidly expanding manufacturing centres – were hated by country people, not simply because "they lost a big market for their horses", but also because of the ugly appearance of the "great raw embankments of the newly-constructed lines". In addition to the dramatic change in the view of Dowles Valley and of Whitehill Road from the river, a small path leading from Lax Lane ford to the Maypole was blocked. "The path lay over a field and was used for carrying corn and flour between the barges and a former windmill which stood not far from the present signal box."

Mrs. Parker related that Mr. Charles Sturge, of the Summerhouse, Wribbenhall,[104] brother of Joseph, "was on the first run of the Stockton and Darlington railway in about 1834". She remembered hearing him describe how coachmen and farmhands threw sticks and stones at the slow-moving train "so that the gentlemen had to stand in front of the ladies to protect them from missiles. The train ran so slowly that the crowd could almost keep up with it. The third class carriages were like trucks with no seats or roofs, so there was little shelter from the stones." Mrs. Parker writes that the new railway from Shrewsbury ran through Mr. Sturge's land, cutting off his road to the town. In recompense, for the period of his lifetime only, he was allowed a footpath and a light bridge over the line.[105]

Charles Sturge had also been one of the guests at the opening of the Liverpool and Manchester Railway in 1830[106] when William Huskisson, one-time Colonial Secretary and leader of the House of Commons, was "accidentally killed by a locomotive engine"[107] – the *Dart*.[108]

The Lamplighter Outside the Wheatsheaf, c1870. Artist's impression: David Edwards, 2003. Reproduced by kind permission of the artist, a former student at the Royal Academy of Arts, London.

Bewdley people must have had serious doubts regarding the railway's advent to their town. Who better to sympathise and reassure them than such philanthropic families as these, who had suffered personal distress and inconvenience in the name of progress.

Happily, the need to diversify in order to survive does not seem to have arisen for the proprietors of the ***Wheatsheaf***. The inn continued to run until ***c1875*** when **Edward Pease**, Esq. purchased it. Two years later, as noted elsewhere, he gave the premises and other buildings on the site to the town as Bewdley Institute.

On 26th February **1862 Mr. Pease had married Sarah Sturge**, daughter of Charles Sturge, former cornfactor of Wribbenhall,[109] and Mary Darby Sturge, whose family came from Coalbrookdale.[110] Edward's grandfather was a *railway projector* who had been helped in his work by two of his sons, Edward's father and his uncle Henry. This same Uncle Henry Pease (1807-1881) had accompanied Sarah's Uncle Joseph Sturge (1793-1859) on a Peace Mission to Russia in 1854.[111]

Perhaps Edward had come to know and love the Bewdley area – and Sarah – through strong family connections such as these, which arose via the Society of Friends, business interests and mutual links with railways.

APPENDIX:

SOME OF THE WHEATSHEAF'S

OTHER ROLES

In addition to its role as an inn, the **Wheatsheaf** – like the **George** – played a central part in the cultural life of the town, hosting some events and supporting others.

Balls and *plays* took place on the premises in the 18th and 19th centuries[112] although, unlike the *George* and also the *Angel* in Load Street, perhaps the *Wheatsheaf* could never boast having hosted a play which starred a famous Thespian.[113] Tickets were available for sale at both the *George* and the *Wheatsheaf* for at least one event "at the Theatre in Bewdley,[114] on Monday, February 23rd 1778" at 7.00pm. Seats in the Gallery cost 1s-0d. (5p), in the Pits 2s-0d. (10p) and in the Boxes 3s-0d. (15p) for "a *Concert* of Vocal and Instrumental Music...; a celebrated new *tragedy* by Richard Savage (never performed here) called *Sir Thomas Overbury* (now acting at the Theatre Royal, Covent Garden, to crowded audiences with the greatest applause); and a *farce* called *The lying valet.*"[115]

A *Friendly Society* met at the *Wheatsheaf* in 1754, as did the Dowles Friendly Society in November 1886,[116] after the inn had been incorporated into Bewdley Institute. Isaac Wedley shows links between Friendly Societies, ancient guilds and payments for prayers for the repose of souls after death.[117]

Not least among the *auctions* which took place there was that of the
"**GEORGE INN** and spacious premises in the centre of
Bewdley, Worcestershire,
TO BE SOLD BY AUCTION by J. PERRY,
At the Wheatsheaf Inn, in Bewdley, on Saturday,
The 21st day of May, 1814, precisely at 4 o'clock in the afternoon".[118]

In 1840, when **Thomas Allcott** was innkeeper, Sir Thomas Winnington, Lord of the Manor, held "a *Court Leet and Baron* at the *Wheat Sheaf* (sic) a fortnight before Easter".[119] The *Court Leet* dealt with petty offences and the *Court Baron* with the rights of the Lord of the Manor and tenants.[120] These

Courts for Bewdley were usually held in the Town Hall, built *c*1808 – and, presumably, in the Guild Hall/Court House which preceded it. The only other occasions that a different location was mentioned in the Directories consulted[121] were in 1873 and 1879, when the "court leet" was "held yearly at the *George* Hotel, within three weeks after Easter".

For many years, it seems that at **election time** the Whigs met at the *Wheatsheaf*[122] and the Tories at the *George*.[123] Maybe the *Assembly Room* of the respective inns was their committee room.

There is an old election song about the popular Sir Thomas Winnington (junior) Whig, being chaired by his supporters during the 1850s and 1860s, at which time the *Swan Hotel* at Stourport was the headquarters of the Whig Party.[124] Whether this had been so in 1847 is unclear, but it seems that the prospective candidates of both political Parties were accused of courting the votes of the electorate by wining and dining them at *all* the local pubs in the run-up to the Election that year. The supporters of Sir Thomas (Edward) Winnington, 11/11/1811-13/6/1872, were no exception, having been fêted at the *Wheatsheaf* that year in the large room.[125] Unlucky licensee Ann Allcott and her waitress, Sarah, were among several Bewdley people who had to undergo cross-examination in Court the following March, the judges finding the case proved.[126] In the event, Sir Thomas was defeated by Thomas James Ireland, Tory – by just two votes.

About eight years earlier, a Press item dated 25th January 1839 had berated the young Sir Thomas, Director Skey and other Whigs for excluding a reporter from the *Ten Towns Messenger,* which supported the Tories, from a public meeting of the Liberal electors of Bewdley. The indignation expressed was exacerbated by the fact that Whigs not only purported to uphold the freedom of the Press but also that they had demonstrated their actual *"illiberality"* by excluding the reporter "at the same moment that they were assuming to themselves the exclusive right to be called *Liberals.*" The article made much of the fact that a representative of the *Worcester Chronicle* – which supported the Whigs – had been freely admitted to recent meetings of Conservative electors in Droitwich, Evesham and Kidderminster, although it criticized the "garbled" reports thereof which appeared in that newspaper.[127]

Ann Allcott's Billhead, the Wheatsheaf, 1856.
Reproduced by courtesy of Bewdley Historical Research Group.

NOTES AND REFERENCES

INTRODUCTION: IF ONLY HE COULD SPEAK

[1] Tunnicliffe: A Survey of the County of Worcester, 1788 – referred to hereafter in this text as 'Tunnicliffe, 1788'.

[2] Institute Annual Report, 1906.

CHAPTER 1: A BRIEF HISTORY OF BEWDLEY'S WHEATSHEAF INN

[3] Although Thomas Weaver (senior) had inherited the premises from his mother, Elizabeth Newey, widow of baker Thomas Newey, it is difficult to ascertain whether the premises had been a bakery before *c*1693.

[4] Gilbert, Don: 'Bewdley Before 1660' in Bewdley in its Golden Age, vol. i: Life in Bewdley 1660-1760. Bewdley Historical Research Group,1991, p.6 – referred to hereafter in this text as 'Bewdley in its Golden Age, i.'.

[5] A Friendly Society met there in 1754. *Source:* Manor Court Records and Vaughan, Terry; Jennings, Jackie; and Park, Betty: 'Inns and Innkeepers' in Bewdley in its Golden Age, i, p.85. Friendly Societies evolved from ancient institutions which were founded for purposes of general well-being. Members paid in regular contributions and the money was used to provide mutual help in times of trouble, e.g. sickness, death. Isaac Wedley shows that such Societies had similar objectives to those of the mediaeval trade guilds. *Source:* Wedley: Kidderminster and its Borderland. *Kidderminster Shuttle*, 1936, p.61 and Bewdley and its Surroundings. *Kidderminster Shuttle*, 1914, p.31.

In his book *The Local Historian's Encyclopedia*. (Historical Publications, 2nd ed. 1986, p.82) John Richardson writes that from 1793 the Clerk of the Peace kept registers of Friendly Societies, plus details of their meeting places and rules. He also says that Literary and Scientific Societies (one of which was a forerunner of and later met at Bewdley Institute) had to obtain a licence to hold meetings after the Seditious Societies Act of 1799, but that an Act of 1843 absolved these Societies from payment of rates if they provided a certificate from the *Barrister for Friendly Societies*.

Interestingly, Brian Wright tells us that *the Friendly Society*, established in 1683, was the name of one of the earliest London fire insurance

societies which formed after the Great Fire of London. *Source*: Wright:
The British Fire Mark, 1680-1879. Woodhead-Faulkner, 1982, p.20.

6   Prattinton, Peter (1771-1840*): Collections for a History of Worcestershire.
4 vols. – referred to hereafter in this text as 'Prattinton'. Vol. iv, pp.411,
412, 415, 416 & 418-420 (referring to the year 1735); p.421 (1736); pp.422
& 424 (re one/both Thomas Bodenham/s); pp.411 & 425 (Richard
Northall); and pp.417, 423 & 424 (re Rowland Bowen). From photostat
copies held at Kidderminster Reference Library. *n.b.* The originals have
different page numbers and are held at the Society of Antiquaries of
London. *Short Biographies of the Worthies of Worcestershire/edited by
Edith Ophelia Browne and John Richard Burton (for the authors, E. G.
Humphreys and Wilson & Phillips, 1916, p.84) gives Prattinton's dates as
1776-1845, but these are amended to 1771-1840 by E. A. B. Barnard in
'Some Additional Notes Concerning the Prattinton Collections of
Worcestershire History' in *Transactions of the Worcestershire Archaeological
Society*, vol. viii, 1931, p.68. Mr. Barnard (ibid.) adds that Dr. Prattinton
died on 11th July 1840 and that a complete typed transcript of his Will "is
now deposited at Birmingham Reference Library".

7   H. Sydney Grazebrook (Heraldry of Worcestershire. 2 vols. John
Russell Smith, 1873, p.690) names John Jeffreys (sic) of Blakebrook,
Kidderminster, as High Sheriff of Worcestershire, 1819. Perhaps he
was a descendant of John Jefferys (sic) to whom number 23 was
mortgaged in 1780, about 6 years before his death.

8   When he died in *c*1717 Thomas Weaver's Inventory listed all the rooms
in number 23 as well as the contents thereof, including many of the
tools he would have used in baking. Thus we can deduce that,
internally as well as externally, the upper part of number 23 has
changed very little over the years.

9   *cf* the *George*, whose landlord William Clare (d.1668), was a Gentleman
/Baker.

10   Fisher, R. N. and Pagett, C.M. in Essays Towards a History of Bewdley edited
by Lawrence S. Snell. University of Birmingham Department of Extramural
Studies, (1972), p.63 – referred to hereafter in this text as 'Essays'.

11   Grant, Neil: Stagecoaches. Kestrel Books, 1977, p.(23).

12   Lewis's Directory 1820 (p.277), 'A Brief Account of the Town of Bewdley'.

13   Neal, Geoff: 'Bewdley's Severn Bridges' in *Worcestershire Archaeological
Society Newsletter*, no. 35, Autumn/Winter 1985, pp.16-18.

14   "1808 the Guildhall (standing on the S.W. side of the chapel) and the
buildings round the church are to be taken down." So writes John

Richard Burton in his book: *A History of Bewdley; with Concise Accounts of Some Neighbouring Parishes*. William Reeves, 1883, p.xxxv – referred to hereafter in this text as 'Burton: Bewdley'.

[15] Members of St. Anne's Church, in 1836 Mr. Godsall's seat there was number 51 – fourth row from the back, on the left-hand (north) side of the main aisle – while Mr. Allcott's was number 23 – second row from the back, on the right-hand side of the main aisle. *Source:* Schedule Drawn up by the Town Council of the Borough of Bewdley, 9th November 1836.

[16] Slater's Directory.

[17] Littlebury's Directory.

[18] 1871 Census. Aged 30, John Penn had been born in Stone, Worcestershire, and his wife, Elizabeth, born in Kidderminster, was 27 years old. They had a "general servant" (Eliza Norwood, aged 21, unmarried, born in Highley, Shropshire) and a lodger (James Chesholm, aged 33, unmarried, who was a Piano Forte Tuner, born in London, Middlesex).

[19] Littlebury's Directory.

[20] Post Office Directory 1868.

[21] In his Foreword to the book *Town and Country in the Victorian West Midlands* Stephen Price describes Mr. Everitt as "One of the most accomplished artists represented in the collection of local topographical drawings and paintings at Birmingham Museum & Art Gallery." Mr. Price is a former Bewdley Museum Curator and was Keeper, Local History Department at Birmingham Museum & Art Gallery in 1986 when the book referred to was published.

[22] 1802 beginnings of photography. Improvements in 1819; 1827;1829; 1838; and 1889. *Source:* Encyclopaedia of Dates and Events, edited by L. C. Pascoe. 2nd ed. revised by Brian Phythian, Hodder & Stoughton, 1974.

SOME ADVERTISEMENTS FOR THE SALE OF THE WHEATSHEAF

[23] Prattinton, vol. iii, p.274.

CHAPTER 2: COACHING

[24] Sparkes, Ivan: Stagecoaches and Carriages. Spurbooks, 1975, p.15.

[25] Grant, op. cit., p.(1).

[26] Tarr, Laszlo; The History of the Carriage. Vision, 1969, p.214.

27 Dymond, Roger: 'Post and Mail Coaches' in *The Guild of Model Wheelwrights' Magazine* (n.d.), but on the internet at www.guildofmodelwheelwrights.org /newsite03/magazine/PostandMailCoaches.htm on 17/9/06.

28 Grant: op. cit., p.(1).

29 Sparkes: op. cit., p.26.

30 Bewdley evidently produced its share of these in the Carters, who were hanged for highway robbery in 1833 (Date and Press details are given by Scaplehorn, Alan: 'James and Joseph Carter' in *Bewdley Civic Society Newsletter*, Autumn 2009, pp.6-7). Wedley relates that the Carters were brought back to be buried at Ribbesford, giving rise to the rumour that they were not buried there at all, their coffin simply being filled with stones. The rumour was subsequently disproved. *Source*: Wedley, Isaac: Bewdley and its Surroundings. *Kidderminster Shuttle*, 1914, p.59 – referred to hereafter in this text as 'Wedley: Bewdley'. In 1594 Robert Palmer, of Blockley, "gentleman" had been luckier, being granted a pardon for the same offence. *Source:* 'An Old Digger' (John Noake): Worcestershire Nuggets. Deighton, 1889, p.348.

31 Thomas De Quincey (1785-1859) in *The English Mail Coach and Other Essays* (Dent, 1912, p.3) writes amusingly about the rivalry between the inside and the outside passengers.

32 Grant: op. cit., p.(18).

33 By 1830, when the roads had improved greatly, four horses were the normal rule. *Source:* Grant: op. cit., p.(6).

34 ibid.

35 My calculations from details given in *Directory of Stage Coach Services 1836* compiled by Alan Bates. David & Charles, 1969, p.(6) and Broadfield, Edward: A Guide to Kidderminster and Neighbourhood. W. Hepworth, 1889, p.30. This calculation is borne out in an article 'Coaching Days' by Alan Huskinson, where he writes: "Even long distance coaches were bound to a rigorous schedule of 10 miles (about 16 km) per hour". *Source: The Midlander,* May 1950, being quoted in the *Kidderminster Shuttle* of 12th May 1950.

36 Wright, Geoffrey: Turnpike Roads. Shire Publications, 1992, p.15.

37 Fisher and Pagett in Essays, p.63.

38 Wedley: Bewdley, p.70.

39 Smith, D. J.: Discovering Horse-Drawn Vehicles. Shire Publications, 1994, p.49.

40 Broadfield, Edward: A Guide to Kidderminster and Neighbourhood. W. Hepworth, 1889, p.30 – referred to hereafter in this text as 'Broadfield'.

41 Smith, D. J.: op. cit., p.49.
42 Smith, D. J.: op. cit., p.51.
43 Grant: op. cit., p.(15).
44 It is said that the former *Horn and Trumpet* on the corner of Park Lane, Kidderminster, got its name because the original cutting down to what was believed to have been a practice ground for archery there (Park Butts) was so narrow that each time a horse travelled along it other horses had to be warned of its presence by blasts on a horn. *Source: Broadfield, p.31.* Originally, the approach along Dog Lane into Load Street must have been equally narrow. Could Bewdley's *Horn and Trumpet* have acquired its name in the same way?
45 Broadfield, pp.29-30. Smith, D. J: op. cit., p.49, says that, in London and elsewhere, stagecoach horses were adorned with flowers or ribbons on May Day or to celebrate a great victory, such as that of Trafalgar.
46 Grant: op. cit., p.(23).
47 Broadfield, pp.35-37.
48 Wedley: Bewdley, p.76. On p.65 Wedley recalls the days when newspapers cost 6d. (2.5p) each, arrived just twice a week, "and were read to the waiting customers in the taverns."
49 Parker, Mrs. J. F., née Alice Tangye: 'Some Old Bewdley Recollections – a paper read on 16th February 1944' in *Transactions of the Worcestershire Archaeological Society*, vol. xxi, 1944, p.16. Reprinted by Ebenezer Baylis, 1945 – referred to hereafter in this text as 'Parker, Mrs. J: Some Old Bewdley Recollections'. The coach which John Lewis drove at this time (1815) was evidently not the *Sovereign*, between Worcester and Bewdley, since that service does not appear to have been started until 1823 (see p.26).

SOME PRESS CUTTINGS ABOUT HIGHWAYMEN, ROAD CONDITIONS, ETC.

50 p.20, *Bewdley Press Cuttings, 18th and early 19th century* bound, typed version at Kidderminster Library – referred to hereafter in this text as '*Bewdley Press Cuttings*'. All cuttings are without titles, unfortunately. I could find no mention of this item in either *Berrow's Worcester Journal* or in the *Weekly Worcester Journal*, despite searching from 17th August to 7th September 1774.
51 *Bewdley Press Cuttings*, p.9. The section of *Berrow's Journal* covering 18th June to 2nd July 1789 was missing from the microfilm and I could not find another newspaper of that date to search at the Record Office.

52 Smith, Captain Alexander: A Complete History of the Lives and Robberies of the Most Notorious Highwaymen, Footpads, Shoplifts, & Cheats of Both Sexes. Routledge & Sons, 1926 (popular edition 1933, edited by Arthur L. Hayward), pp.447-453.

CHAPTER 3: COACHING IN BEWDLEY BEFORE 1835

53 Vaughan, Jennings and Park <u>in</u> Bewdley in its Golden Age, i, p.86.
54 Probably number 6 Severnside (South). *Source:* ibid.
55 Finch, D. J: The Impact of Transport Systems on the Development of Bewdley, Kidderminster and Stourport between 1660 and 1880; with a Particular Focus on the Years 1770-1880. Unpublished Dissertation, Worcester College of Higher Education, 1990, pp.2 & 3. A copy is held at Kidderminster Reference Library.
56 *Bewdley Press Cuttings*, p.11.
57 op. cit., p.12.
58 Only wealthy people travelled by coach until the early 18th century. Everyone else had to walk, or go on horseback or by the then uncomfortable and fairly slow wagons pulled by heavy horses. *Source:* Young, Rosa: 'Following the Stagecoaches' <u>in</u> *The Local Historian*, <u>14</u> (6) May 1981, p.342. The wheels on wagons seemed to be especially broad, and therefore heavy, to cope with the uneven road surfaces. *Source:* Wright, Geoffrey N: Turnpike Roads, p.5. No wonder they travelled fairly slowly. Fortunately roads and wagon design had improved by the time of the local *Flying Wagons*.
59 *Bewdley Press Cuttings*, p.14.
60 op. cit., p.13. No year is given, but during John Crump's period at the *George*. Kenneth Hobson writes that Crump purchased the freehold in 1777, but was a tenant as far back as 1755. *Source:* A History of the George Hotel, Load Street, Bewdley. Winwood Design & Print agency/Norman Hills Print, 1994, pp.2, 6 & 4 – referred to hereafter in this text as 'Hobson, K: The George Hotel'.
61 Prattinton, vol. iv, p.401.
62 *Bewdley Press Cuttings*, p.12.
63 op. cit., p.14.
64 op. cit., p.15.
65 Bates 1836 Directory records Thomas Waddell & Co.'s coaches also running between <u>Birmingham and Bristol</u>, "1 single journey, Monday to Saturday"; <u>Birmingham and Derby</u>, "1 return journey, Monday to

Coaching and the Wheatsheaf Inn

Saturday"; <u>Birmingham and Shrewsbury</u>, "1 return journey daily"; <u>Birmingham and Yarmouth</u>, "1 single journey daily"; and <u>Birmingham and Manchester</u>, "1 single journey, Monday to Saturday". *Source*: Directory of Stage Coach Services 1836, compiled by Alan Bates. David & Charles, 1969, pp. 89, 91, 92 & 115 – referred to hereafter in this text as 'Bates 1836 Directory'.

66 In 1836 H. Godfrey & Co. ran a coach between <u>Birmingham and Kidderminster</u>, "1 single journey daily" and between <u>Ludlow and Brimfield</u>, "1 single journey, Monday to Saturday". *Source:* Bates 1836 Directory, pp.90 & 113.

67 Was this the same firm as C. Radenhurst & Co. who ran coaches between <u>Birmingham and Kidderminster</u>; <u>Birmingham and Leicester</u>; and <u>Kidderminster and Brecon</u>? Radenhurst & Co., perhaps C. Radenhurst, plied between <u>Birmingham and Birkenhead</u> in 1836. *Source:* Bates 1836 Directory, pp.89, 90, 108.

68 The fares recorded on the handbill by Dr. Prattinton are: "Emerald, outside £1-4s-6d. (£1.22½); inside £2-7s-6d. (£2.37½)". Mr. Barnard presumes these were the prices for the through journey from Stourbridge to London by this coach.

CHAPTER 4: THE HEYDAY OF COACHING AT THE WHEATSHEAF

69 Broadfield, p.27.
70 Hobson, K: The George Hotel, pp.4 & 5.
71 Bentley's Directory.
72 Bates 1836 Directory, p.136.
73 Bates: op. cit., p.(iv).
74 Parker, Mrs. J: Some Old Bewdley Recollections, p.16. One can sympathise with Old William (the narrator, in Wedley: Bewdley, pp.19-20 & Errata p.(xiv)) who, shocked at the realisation of time's onward march says to his companion, "I see old John Lewis's name on the door (of some neglected buildings facing the Severn). ... Lewis drove the old coach to Worcester, but, by the look of these premises, their interest in Wribbenhall is gone."
75 In *Some Old Bewdley Recollections* (p.16) Mrs. Parker writes that he was born in 1791 and died in 1893, but in *Old Bewdley and its Industries* (Reprinted from the *Transactions of the Worcestershire Archaeological Society* for 1932, p.18) she says, "Mr. Lewis died in 1882, aged 101."
76 The Severn Valley Railway was officially opened on 31st January 1862. *Source:* Fisher and Pagett: <u>in</u> Essays, p.79.

77 Bates 1836 Directory makes no reference to Thomas Ree but *does* list T. *Reeves* & Co., pp. 92 & 137. Not mentioned in Lewis's 1820 Directory under *Bewdley*, Thomas and Edward Ree were recorded at the *George*, Bewdley, in Pigot's Directory for 1830, this being the next Directory available. The Ree family were still recorded there in 1840 (Bentley's Directory), but had evidently left the *George* by 1842 (Pigot's Directory). If T. Ree and T. Reeves were the same person, then his coaching business had expanded before he retired, for in 1836 the firm served: Birmingham and Worcester, "1 return journey Monday to Saturday, Licence number 7577, 4 passengers inside and 8 outside"; Worcester and Leominster, "1 return journey Tuesday, Thursday & Saturday, Licence number 7630, 4 passengers inside and 5 outside"; and Worcester and Hereford, "1 return journey Monday to Saturday, Licence numbers 7631, 7632, 4 passengers inside and 8 outside".

78 Bates 1836 Directory, pp.60 & 73.

79 op. cit., p.82.

80 op. cit., pp.86, 104 & 107 list J. Barnet/J. Barnett & Co. also running coaches between Abergavenny and Monmouth Cap, "12 miles, 1 return journey on Tuesday only"; Gloucester and Dursley, "15 miles, 1 return journey, Monday, Wednesday and Saturday"; Hereford and Abergavenny, "24 miles, 1 return journey, Monday to Saturday"; and Hereford and Monmouth Cap, "12 miles, 1 return journey, Saturday only."

81 Curiously, a *J. Gardener* ran a coach between Worcester and Kidderminster and between Kidderminster and Stourbridge in 1836. *Source:* Bates 1836 Directory, pp.137 & 108.

82 Billing's Directory.

83 ibid.

84 Slater's Directory.

85 From 1784 to 1874 a tax was levied on the possession of horses. *Source:* Richardson, John: The Local Historian's Encyclopedia. Historical Publications, 2nd ed. 1986, p.48 – referred to hereafter in this text as 'Richardson'.

86 Littlebury's Directory.

87 Kelly's Directory.

88 Census.

89 House number 17, according to Kelly's Directory 1892.

90 Several years earlier, in 1836, coaches were usually owned and maintained by *coach builders* and were hired out to *coach proprietors* on a mileage basis. *Source:* Bates 1836 Directory, p.(iii).

91 Haughton, Brian: Coaching Days in the Midlands. Quercus, 1997, pp.110 & 111.

92 Although Mr. Charles Sturge's *Diary* (1840-1850) noted: "There was still a good trade on the river. With a strong south wind blowing, flat-bottomed barges, each carrying sixty tons, might be seen going up stream with large white square sails spread to aid the towing horses." *Source:* Parker, Mrs. J: Old Bewdley and its Industries, p.18.

93 Fisher and Pagett <u>in</u> Essays, pp.78-79.

94 Finch: op. cit., p.41.Tomkinson, K. and Hall, G: Kidderminster Since 1800. Kenneth Tomkinson, 2nd ed. 1985, p.165, says this was the first 36 miles (about 57.6 kilometres) of the Oxford, Worcester and Wolverhampton Railway to be opened.

95 Finch: op. cit., p.41.

96 Burton: Bewdley, p.83.

97 op. cit., p.10.

98 Pardoe, Bill: Witley Court and Church: Life in a Great Country House. Peter Huxtable Designs Ltd., 1986, p.1.

99 Peckover, Alexandrina: Life of Joseph Sturge. Sonnenschein, 2nd ed., n.d. but after 1890 – the date of the 1st edition. Interestingly, in her booklet *Two Brothers*, p.5 (Reprinted from the *Kidderminster Times*, 11th May 1946), Mrs. Parker says that a Mr. Peckover attempted, unsuccessfully, to obtain coal from the Dowles Valley in *c*1879 and that the bore-hole could still be seen from the bridge in 1946.

100 Short Biographies of the Worthies of Worcestershire, edited by Edith Ophelia Browne and John Richard Burton (for the authors, E. G. Humphreys and Wilson & Phillips, 1916, p.158) – referred to hereafter in this text as 'Worthies of Worcestershire'.

101 Dictionary of National Biography (D.N.B.). Smith, Elder & Co., 1885-1900 (63 vols.).

102 Headstone, Quaker Burial Ground, Lower Park, Bewdley.

103 Parker, Mrs. J. F.: The Roads Through Bewdley. Printed by the *Kidderminster Times*, n.d. but probably between *c*1920s and 1940s, p.6 – referred to hereafter in this text as 'Parker, Mrs. J: The Roads Through Bewdley'.

104 In *Some Old Bewdley Recollections* Mrs. Parker tells of the transformation of one of four former gazebos in the town into the house which is known nowadays as the **Summer *House***, but evidently as **Summer *Hill*** in the 1851 and 1861 Censuses, in various Directories of that decade and on an Ordnance Survey map of 1884. She writes that **Benjamin Cotterell***

(wharfinger, who died in *c*1778) bought a cave that overlooked the town and built a **summerhouse** over it for a picnic room. Later owners extended it at various times, "and the house exists today (1944) as the **Summer House**". *Source*: Parker in *Transactions of the Worcestershire Archaeological Society,* vol. xxi, 1944, pp. 17 & 19. *Although, "Historians are divided as to whether it was Benjamin Cotterill/Cotterell or William Harwood who, in (*c*)1740... built a summer-house... in Wribbenhall." *Source:* Purcell, Angela; Purcell, Charles; & Hobson, Kenneth: Bewdley's Past in Pictures, vol. ii. Bewdley Historical Research Group, 1996, p.68. I have not yet discovered whether **Benjamin Cotterell** was related to **H. F. Cotterell**, former partner of Charles Sturge's brother – **Joseph Sturge** (1793-1859), cornfactor in Bewdley from *c*1814-1822 – but it is interesting to note some associations of people and places over the years: • **John Lewis,** coachman, lived in a Georgian house which was owned by **Benjamin Cotterell**, wharfinger, and which appears to have been close to the ***Dog Wheel***, Wribbenhall. *(The **Dog Wheel** was so named because a dog running inside a wheel turned a spit to roast meat evenly).* • As a girl, Mrs. J. F. Parker (*c*1873-1960) had attended Miss Puckey's school in the building which later became known as the Homestead and then, as now, the ***Dog Wheel***, Wribbenhall. *Source:* B.H.R.G. File 3, no.18, p.16; • the ***Dog Wheel*** was the one-time home of **George Griffith**, traveller for **Charles Sturge**. The Sturges' warehouses adjoined the *Dog Wheel* at that time. *Source:* Griffith, G: Going to Markets and Grammar Schools. William Freeman, 1870 (2 vols.), vol. i, p.134. • Wedley: Bewdley (p.21) writes that **George Griffith** sold the ***Dog Wheel*** to the Puckeys. **Matthew Puckey**, who became Inland Revenue Officer at the *Wheatsheaf* lived at the ***Dog Wheel*** in 1855. • Between *c*1896 and March 1901, Directories show that ***J(ohn) A(ffleck) Bridges***, who wrote rather scathingly about **George Griffith**, *lived at Summer Hill,* former home of **Charles Sturge**.

105 Parker, Mrs. J: The Roads Through Bewdley, pp.6-7.

106 Charles Sturge seems to have been a very gallant gentleman, for twice in the 1830s he protected ladies from missiles. On this occasion he and others "crowded in front of the ladies on the Liverpool/Manchester train to protect them and their gala dresses" from stones and mud being hurled by an angry mob at the Duke of Wellington, who was also on the train. *Worthies of Worcestershire,* p.157, relates how the Duke was unpopular because of the Corn Laws, which put taxes on bread.

107 Worthies of Worcestershire, pp.157 & 81.

108 D.N.B.

[109] *The British Friend,* 1862, p.71. (Courtesy of Darlington Library & Art Gallery).

[110] Née Dickinson, born in *c*1807, Mary Darby Sturge was a Darby of Coalbrookdale. *Sources:* D.N.B. and B.H.R.G. File 3, no. 18, p.22, respectively. Another link between the two might have been through the family woollen manufacturing business of Messrs. H. **Pease** & Co. in Darlington which was contemporary with, although longer-established than, Henry **Sturge**'s Bewdley carpet factory, founded in *c*1825. *Sources: Northern Echo,* 21st June 1989 and 14th June 1880 (Courtesy of Darlington Library & Art Gallery) – re H. Pease & Co.; and Parker, Mrs. J: *Old Bewdley and its Industries,* p.18 – re Henry Sturge.

[111] They were kindly received, but later events meant that their attempts to dissuade that country from taking part in the then imminent Crimean War were unsuccessful.

APPENDIX: SOME OF THE WHEATSHEAF'S OTHER ROLES

[112] Vaughan, Jennings and Park in Bewdley in its Golden Age, i, p.80.

[113] Sarah Siddons (1755-1831) is reputed to have played in the Assembly Hall at the *George* and at the *Angel. Respective sources:* Hobson, K: The George Hotel, p.3 and Wedley: Bewdley, p.22 and also indicated on the Contents Page under a summary of Chapter viii.

[114] Was "the Theatre in Bewdley" a barn at the back of the *Angel,* Load Street, which was regularly used as a theatre in the 18th century? *Source:* Vaughan, Jennings and Park in Bewdley in its Golden Age, i, p.84.

[115] *Bewdley Press Cuttings,* pp.34 & 35.

[116] *Bewdley Parish Magazine,* 1886 reproduced by Nigel Knowles. Star & Garter Publishers, 1997, p.116.

[117] *cf* the chantries in the 15th century wooden chapel which was directly opposite number 23 until *c*1745; the Buttercross, east of the chapel, which was rebuilt in 1632 – the same date as appears on the cross-beam of number 23; and Bewdley's first known bridge, built in 1447. I have explored this comparison further in my forthcoming book *Over Agaynst the Chappell; 21-23 Load Street, Bewdley – the Buildings and Occupants from c1632 to c1875. See also* Ref. 5, above.

[118] *The Worcester Herald,* 7th May 1814.

[119] Bentley's Directory.

[120] Shorter Oxford English Dictionary on Historical Principles (S.O.E.D.). Prepared by William Little, H. W. Fowler and J. Coulson. Revised & edited by C. T. Onions. 3rd rev. ed., O.U.P., 1955 and Richardson, p.32.

In *Bewdley and its Surroundings* (pp.78/79) Wedley describes the ceremony of the Court Leet, as seen through the eyes of the book's narrator, Old William.

121 Bewdley section of Worcestershire Directories consulted: (handwritten) Bailey's **1783**; Tunnicliffe's **1788**; Universal British **1793** & **1798/99**; Holden's Triennial **1805/1806/1807** & **1809/1810/1811**; (printed) Lewis's General & Commercial **1820**; Pigot's **1830, 1835** & *c***1835**; Bentley's **1840**; Pigot's **1842**; Slater's **1850**; Billing's **1855**; Cassey's **1860**; Slater's **1862**; Post Office **1863, 1868** & **1876**; Littlebury's **1873** & **1879**; Kelly's **1884, 1892** & **1896**; Court Guide **1902**; Kelly's **1904, 1912, 1916, 1924, 1928, 1932** & **1940**.

122 Although evidently not averse to using the *Assembly Room* of the 'opposition' for non-political purposes. e.g. Two of the three *Stewards* at "the last **Bewdley Assembly** this winter... at the *George*" on 6th March 1823 were Sir T. E. Winnington (senior), Whig, and Lady Winnington, who was also Lady Patroness. *Source: Bewdley Press Cuttings*, p.40.

123 Hobson, K: The George Hotel, p.6. It was certainly so in 1847. *Source:* Minutes of Evidence Taken Before the Select Committee on the Bewdley Election Petition, 1848. *Ordered, by* the House of Commons, *to be Printed*, 22 March 1848, pp.19, 85-99, 146-156 & 275-287 – referred to hereafter in this text as 'Minutes of Evidence, 1848'.

124 Wedley, I. L: Old Stourport. *Kidderminster Shuttle*, 1912, p.5. Father and son, both Whigs, shared the name *Thomas Edward Winnington*. The election song about the popular Thomas Winnington refers to the son (1811-1872) rather than to the father (d.1839). *Source* for dates of the two Thomas Edward Winningtons – Williams, W(illiam) R(etlaw): The Parliamentary History of the County of Worcester. The author, 1897, p.175.

125 Two rooms led off the large room, one of these being the committee room which had once been used as a bedroom. The large room seems to have been the ballroom and was upstairs at the back of the house. It had two doors and a fireplace. The hustings were only about 30 or 40 yards (approx. 27 or 36 metres) from the *Wheatsheaf*.

126 Minutes of Evidence, 1848, pp.275-287.

127 *Bewdley Press Cuttings*, p.43.